Rail Ramble Round Ireland, July 1969
Hugh Dougherty

Progress along the street on the Cork City Railways; a man in front waves traffic aside with the train in full cry behind.

© Hugh Dougherty, 2023
First published in the United Kingdom, 2023,
by Stenlake Publishing Ltd.
54-58 Mill Square,
Catrine, KA5 6RD
01290 551122
www.stenlake.co.uk

ISBN 978-1-84033-959-8

The publishers regret that they cannot supply copies of any pictures featured in this book.

Printed by
P2D Books, 1 Newlands Rd,
Westoning, Bedford MK45 5LD

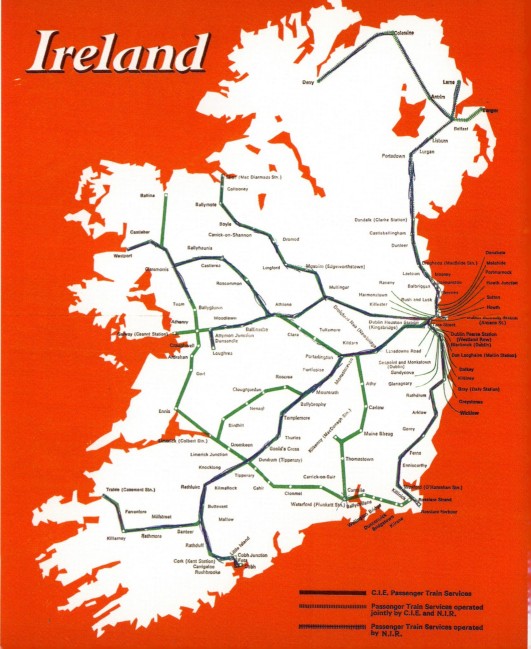

The map from the 1969 summer timetable with the routes taken marked in biro.

Monday 7th July: Off To Dublin on the train, on the train!

It's Monday 7th July 1969, and I'd left my parent's holiday home in Laghey, outside Donegal Town, with, hopefully, enough cash in my wallet, the proceeds of student holiday jobs, and caught the CIE bus on the joint County Donegal Railways route for Sligo.

My 18 year-old, nervous excitement was rising as we pulled into Bundoran's ex-Great Northern Railway of Ireland Bus Depot, beside the cruelly abandoned station at which I'd arrived from Belfast in 1957. That magical, steam-driven journey, was never forgotten, and, now I was off to see as much of surviving Irish railways as I could.

I was looking forward to exploring the CIE railway system, of which I'd read, but not seen or ridden on, knowing only Donegal and Northern Ireland. Not only that, but I was away on my own for the first time, free of parents, free to roam, and just slightly nervous!

Would my money last? No cards or ATMs in those days and, just in case everyone's forgotten, in that pre-digital age off you went, without a mobile phone, social media or anything else. My parents didn't expect to hear from me, unless of course in an emergency, unlike today when constant tweets and texts tell you where everyone is. The sense of distance and adventure was much, much, greater in 1969. I was ready for it.

So, off the familiar bus, a CIE C Class Leyland Leopard, complete with airbag suspension, which wasn't great on Donegal roads, at Sligo Station, where buses terminated in a brave show of integrated transport. With a mixture of pride and, I suppose, fear, I made for the ticket office, for this was crossing the threshold into unknown territory for a Glasgow-Donegal man like me, to head south into the heart of the Republic, where Donegal was viewed as remote. And the south, unlike Donegal by 1969, was a country with miles of highly-functioning railways, even if many of its gems, such as the Cavan & Leitrim, Tralee & Dingle, West Clare and the West Cork lines had, by that time, fallen to the accountant's axe.

Advert for Rambler Tickets from the 1969 summer timetable.

Sligo MacDiarmada Station, named in 1966, after Sean MacDiarmada, one of the Irish patriots of Easter 1916, looked impressive. Once the terminus of the Midland Great Western Railway from Dublin, the Waterford, Limerick and Western from Limerick itself and, later, part of the Great Southern & Western Railway and the deliciously eccentric Sligo Leitrim & Northern Counties Railway linking Sligo with the GNR(I) at Enniskillen, the building had survived near destruction during the Civil War. Here was history all around and the romantic 18-year-old me could touch the past!

Into the booking office, to ask for a CIE Rail Rambler Ticket, which, for £9, and remember that Ireland used Sterling in those far-off times, entitled you to travel across the CIE network for two weeks. The cost was almost a week's pay in my bus conductor student holiday job, but still good value. The booking clerk who sold me the ticket was really interested as to where I'd get to. It turned out that he was a CIE graduate trainee, doing a stint in booking offices. *"By the time I've finished,"* he said in his flat, Dublin accent, *"I'll have done just about every job on the railway. It's wonderful. You should think about it yourself when you graduate."*

At the platform, the 15.05, with buffet car, was waiting to leave for Dublin, which suddenly felt quite daunting and very far away from Donegal. I thought, for a moment of forgetting the whole thing. I could just get the next Derry bus from outside the station, and be home in Laghey in time for tea in front of our turf fire with the mother and father. But I dismissed that quickly and tingled slightly. This was the adventure of a lifetime. Never mind that hippies were travelling to India and fellow students were buzzing around the world on jets: Sligo to Dublin was enough for me!

My train was made up of CIE AEC railcars, dating from the early 1950s, and almost identical to the GNR(I) cars that I'd travelled on from Belfast to Omagh, for Bundoran, after they'd shut the Enniskillen and Bundoran lines in September 1957. There was a comforting feeling of familiarity. The platform was bustling, as more bus connections arrived, and luggage, mail and parcels were being loaded into the guard's van. The train's importance, the 1969-version in my mind of one the dashing Midland Great Western Railway Expresses of which I'd read in OS Nock's classic book, *The Trains We Loved*, was underlined by the fact that it boasted a buffet car, staffed by a white-jacketed, catering crew, one of whom was hanging out an open window smoking furiously as he surveyed the scene.

Miniature train staff for the single line, duly delivered to the guard by the Sligo signalman, a whistle blowing, a green flag waving, and the busy, black-and-tan livered, railcar set eased out of Sligo, a terminal strangely empty without its former terminating WL&W and SL&NCR trains, and I was on my way.

Past the Sligo Quay Branch, which still handled a healthy goods traffic, the station's large signal cabin and engine shed, boasting steam era turntable and water tank we went, to the business-like sound of AEC engines. Their melodious, Wilson epicyclical gear changes and the clatter of wheels on the jointed track – no welded Sligo Road in those days – gave the impression that we were railwaying in the traditional sense. And we were.

Sligo Station from the buffer stops where the great adventure started on Monday 7th July 1969.

A goods train comes up the Sligo Quay line with Ben Bulben in the background.

On these railcars, if you could blag a seat behind the driver's cab, you would see him at work on the gear preselector lever, moving it before thumping it into gear with the hand-operated clutch control, and pressing the foot-operated throttle, to pick up speed. It was sophisticated for its time, but would be unrecognisable to Iarnrod Eireann drivers on the Sligo line railcar sets today, with their combined brake and power control, electronic wonders and radio contact systems.

A quick look back at Ben Bulbin, and then out with my 1969 timetable, which, cost 4d, but which my friends in the County Donegal Railways Office at Stranorlar had managed to blag for me for free before I left, to plan the days ahead. There were some butterflies in my tummy, but this was Irish railways in action. I was captivated.

To guide me on my way, apart from some fervent prayers to St Columcille, to lead me safely back to Donegal (!), I had my own 'bible' in the shape of *Irish Railways Today*, a marvellous book, published in 1967 by Transport Research Associates of Dublin. In it, authors Brendan Pender and Herbert Richards detailed all lines still open, describing every feature and giving a potted history too, with notes, on locomotives and rolling stock of both CIE and Northern Ireland Railways. With all of this, and my timetable, I was in business.

In my awkward suitcacse of the time, for remember that this was long before the ergonomic backpacks of today or the wheeled luggage that make travel so much easier, was also my new, Kodak 133, Instamatic camera, bought at enormous cost, so it seemed, as a penniless student, for £6.00. With its fixed focus lens, two settings, normal and bright, and a flash cube slot on top, it was much better than the camera of unknown lineage I'd bought for 4/6 in Buncrana a few years before, and which I used for my early shots of CDR and Lough Swilly buses. I had that along, too, for black and white shots, and just in case.

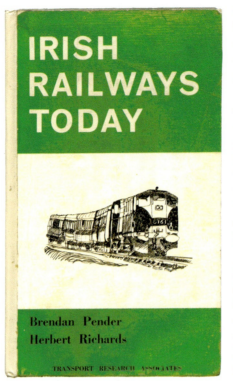

The 133 took 24-shot, 126 slide film cartridges, and I had three of these to last my whole time, so, every shot had to count. The real thrill was sending the films off to Kodak in the yellow, red and white envelops that came with each film, and receiving your processed slides back a few days later. They even came to your address in the Republic carrying a green, customs declaration, as the Kodak lab was in England. Ah, the thrill of it all, then!

But back to the railcar train for Dublin. Using *Irish Railways Today*, I picked up the junction at Carrignagat for the closed Sligo Leitrim line, and at Collooney for what crews called the Burma Road, south towards Claremorris, then still open for goods, and tuned into the gear changes and healthy engine cacophony, as we climbed over the shoulder of the Ox Mountains.

At stations, the guard exchanged the miniature train staffs with the signalman, and it was interesting to see that very little had changed since steam days on CIE in 1969. There was full semaphore signalling, water tanks and cranes much in evidence, loose-coupled goods trains, made up of wagons without continuous brakes, with cattle and mail trains, too. Turntables were in use at major stations, essential for turning the single-ended General Motors B class locos, which handled much of the traffic with aplomb, and there were plenty of staff around to deal with parcels, newspapers, sundries and mails. This was a very traditional railway by any standards.

But, back on board, the ticket collector looked at my ticket, and, much to my surprise clipped it, as though it had been an ordinary single or return. I could see me having very little, legible ticket left by the end of my time on the rails, but, thankfully, most of his colleagues, subsequently just nodded and had a chat about where I was going to get to!

We crossed the up train, another railcar set, at Dromod, where I tried in vain to spot anything of the Cavan & Leitrim Railway, closed in 1959, and long before, courtesy of preservationist, Michael Kennedy, railway sounds came back to the station's narrow gauge yard. Just before Dromod, we drummed across the opening bridge over the River Shannon, and, as my book told me, all along the route, passed former junctions with long-closed branch lines.

I was clad in teeshirt and light, summer trousers, but most people, in 1969, were dressed in their best to travel: ladies in suits, or costumes, as some called them, gents in tweedy suits, some of great vintage, and not a few wearing flat caps. Pioneer Total Abstinence Association pins were much in evidence. There was a selection of nuns and priests travelling, for this was still very much De Valera's Catholic Ireland and, of course, there was smoking galore, but not the nuns as I recall….

Heavy suitcases took up space on the luggage racks, and, as we headed south east, through Longford, more passengers boarded. Opposite me, came on an older gent, who to me looked ancient, but he soon proved himself of great interest as he chatted about his exploits as an IRA fighter during the War of Independence. And when the guard came round for his ticket, he proudly took out his veteran's pass, which gave him free rail travel, stopping to let me see it, and one of his medals, as he exhorted me, as he said, a young Irishman, to fight for a united Ireland.

Running down alongside Lough Owel, and nearing Mullingar, it was clear that the track was in need of some TLC, for the noise created by corrugations, better known was 'roaring rails' was deafening in parts, and the train, seemed to be travelling much faster than it was. Efficient as it was, the CIE railway needed

Cover of the battleworn ticket punctured by its many clippings.

investment by 1969, and that was subject to great Government debate. The future was far from secure, even though the core network was intact.

At Mullingar, we ticked over by the platform, as the M&GWR main line west to Galway, kicked in. A wheeltapper, slinging his hammer with ease, ensured that our wheels rang true, while passengers got on and off, and, with just 50 miles, to go, Dublin started to seem much nearer.

We sped off for the capital with great purpose over what had been the Midland's racing track, following the banks of the adjacent Royal Canal, roaring through stations such as Enfield, Killucan and Maynooth, through the loops in top gear as the guard worked the automatic, train staff exchange snatcher, using a roll-down shutter

Down in Dublin, a CIE AEC railcar set waits its time at Connolly Station.

A B Class loco is swung around on the Connolly turntable. Turntables were in common use on CIE in 1969.

aperture beside his van, and belling the driver to confirm a successful exchange. The outgoing staff was picked up by the same ground apparatus as had delivered the staff taken on board. It was purposeful, precise and fascinating to watch, adding considerably to the character of the trip.

And so, into what was then Dear, Dirty Dublin, which struck me as very busy and very like an English city, and far from home. I stayed on past Connolly to get out at Pearse, former Westland Row Station, where the train terminated, and took stock.

It was 18.40, the rush hour was over, and a single-ended, B class diesel sat in the other road, under Pearse's impressive overall roof, turning over with the distinctive beat of its General Motors engine. It seemed to speak of lines yet to be explored and to be beckoning me to go further. But, I was bound for an 11 bus, to the North Circular Road, where I'd booked up a B&B via the Bord Failte tourist office at Donegal Town, who did all the phoning for you – this was the days before the internet – and made my way there.

The CIE buses of that era in Dublin were full of character, old wonderfully-smooth, blue-and-cream, double-decker, Leylands with rear platform and conductors wielding their TIM ticket machines with ease, regardless of how busy their bus was. The Leylands shared Dublin's crowded road space with the last double deckers, the RA class, built at the old GNR works at Dundalk, and almost-new Leyland Atlanteans, all still conductor worked. This was a system which worked, even though the spectre of one man operation was hanging over the city, and my bus got me to my B&B, where I was welcomed by a motherly lady, whose own boys were students.

I felt safe in what seemed a foreign city, very different from Glasgow, and a world away from Donegal. It seems strange in today's travel-hungry and jet-connected world, to recall these thoughts and feelings, over 50 years later, but my prayers that night were for a safe time down south, and I fell asleep to the sound of AEC railcar engines and roaring rails. It had been quite a first day out on the tracks.

A CIE Atlantean makes its way along O'Connell Street as part of the Fair City's efficient bus system. Atlanteans took me to my digs on the North Circular Road.

On O'Connell Street in Dublin, a CIE R class Leyland, with two nuns and a Catholic Truth Society's triangular red portable stall on the right.

The double-header Slainte ready for the off to Cork at Dublin Heuston.

Tuesday 8th July : Mainline to Cork.

I was up early, well-fed on what the landlady told me was a full Ulster Fry, just to make me feel at home (!) on the Tuesday, to catch the bus – no LUAS trams in those days – to Heuston Station, formerly Kingsbridge, and named after 1916 patriot, Sean Heuston, for the 08.45 departure, down the Great Southern & Western Railway to Cork.

This was the real deal in the shape of the Slainte – Irish for 'Welcome' – Cork express, non-stop to Limerick Junction, and into Cork for 11.35, calling for smart running by the single-ended and doubled-ended 'B' class, General Motors diesels, running in multiple, which I duly photographed as they ticked over purposefully. Boarding the Cravens coaches were businessmen and women in plenty, while a smartly-uniformed CIE rail hostess, shepherded folk aboard. This was a crack express on a real, Irish main line railway, and I was up for it. The thrill of having so many miles of track and new places in front of me was palpable: in those days you couldn't look up a website to see what Cork looked like or to learn all that there was to learn about the trains before you got there. I can't help feeling that we've lost a great deal and that much of the mystery and romance of rail has gone.

Away, right on time, out of Heuston and past Inchicore Works, another target on my hit list, and out into the flat Curragh of Kildare, the locos fairly sizzling away at the head of our train, as we ramped up speed into the high 70s. All around the line were rich, green fields, rather larger than those in Donegal, and the 107 miles to Limerick Junction, that famous spot which required through trains to and from Cork to reverse into the platform, and face the outgoing service, flew past. Arrival at the junction was spot on, at 10.30. Quite a few got off to pick up the connection to Limerick, and, peckish, after my early breakfast, I headed for the dining car, a superb, 12-wheeled, ex G&SWR, clerestory-roofed specimen, that was riding along with a regal smoothness.

Sitting at a table, a white-jacketed member of the catering crew took my order for tea and soda bread with jam and butter, the jam coming in a tiny, plastic, portion pot, with "CIE Catering Services" on its lid. The teapot was ex-Great Southern Railway, the plate, cup and saucer CIE and the knife ex-Great Northern Railway. If only I had blagged some of it! It would be worth a fortune today.

It was memorable to eat at a table laid with a white cloth, as the train headed on towards Mallow, and there was a feeling of tapping into something timeless and almost Victorian, as the restaurant car sedately ran along over well-maintained, but jointed track. Out of the window, the rise and fall of the telephone wires was clear, dipping as they seemed to collide with each, passing, telegraph pole. All that was missing were wisps of steam, as I conjured up the image of one of the massive 4-6-0s, built for the Cork expresses by the GSR, perhaps *Maeve* herself, by 1969, safely preserved in the Belfast Transport Museum, at the head of our train.

However, when I got up to pay my bill at the counter, all was not well. I can't remember the price of my snack, but the steward, clearly mistaking me for a naive young lad, or worst still, a daft tourist, failed to ring up the cost on his TIM ticket machine used for issuing receipts, and produced an already-issued ticket from under the machine. Even the value was wrong!

"Can you please give me a receipt from the machine," I asked courteously. *"That's an old one. I'm a bus conductor myself, and I know how these machines work."*

"Are you accusing me of thieving, sir?" With the emphasis on the 'SIR' he spat it out with contempt in a flat, and mocking Dublin accent, as the younger members of the catering crew looked on with great interest.

"You've maybe just made a mistake. Just give me a proper receipt, please."

Chastened, and realising that I wasn't a mug, he issued a ticket for the right amount, and threw it across the counter to me. And, as I turned, I could just make out *"Northern b------ "*, said just so I could hear it, clearly mistaking my Glasgow-Donegal accent as being

On the way down to Cork we passed A8 on a goods train at Portarlington. Traditional goods traffic was still alive and well on CIE.

Cork Kent Station was an impressive place. Note the traditional signalling and the goods avoiding lines to the right.

from the six counties, something that I became used to the further south I went.

It was the one unpleasant episode that happened in all my travels that week and every other member of railway staff I came across was courteous, interested and friendly, especially the driver of the Loughrea Branch train, who invited me up on his footplate for the journey, but more of that anon.

So, on though Mallow, junction for Killarney and Tralee at full tilt, and down past the extensive sidings at Rathpeacon, in 1969, full of wagons, before passing the original terminus of the line at Kilbarry, and plunging down the gradient through the 1,355-yard long Glanmire Tunnel, into Kent Station, and journey's end. We were right on schedule at 11.35, and in good time for the noon Angelus, which was still much observed in public, in the Ireland of 1969.

I had a good look around Kent Station, with its sparkling, black-and-white main platform surfaces, and went out onto the concourse of this through station, which also served the Cobh branch, and, at that time, the Youghal line, then open for summer excursion traffic only.

Kent was busy, but right there, on a pedestal, was the station's famous Bury 2-2-2 loco, number 36, dating from 1848, and still there, today. The loco predated Kent itself, which was custom-built in 1893, and, which in 1969, came complete with loco shed, platform avoiding line, goods yard and connections with Cork Quays on the River Lee. Today's version is still impressive, but much slimmed down from common carrier railway days.

With plenty of time, after stopping for a quick Angelus, along with most other people, on the busy city streets, it was time to take a look around, and I marvelled at the lifting road bridges, complete with inset railway track, which crossed the Lee. These were part of the Cork City Railways, used by freight trains coming from the Albert Quay Station, once terminus of the Cork Bandon & South Coast Railway, with lines to places such as Bantry and Skibereen, and still in use as a freight depot in 1969.23

Sadly the West Cork lines had been closed in 1961. If they had still been open, I'd have made my way out to the south west, but by 1969 all that was on offer was replacement buses operating from Cork's bus station. A quick look there revealed Leyland double deckers, identical to their Dublin cousins, running on city services, with CIE E and C Class Leyland Leopards, on provincial routes, including the rail replacement services to West Cork.

Best then to get some more value out of my ticket, so I headed back to Kent and caught 13.30 to Cobh, even in 1969 known as the last port of call for the doomed *Titanic*, long before the ship that left Belfast in fine condition, as they say up there, reached Hollywood and Belfast tourist attraction fame.

The branch train had a double-ended "B" class General Motors loco, B147 which had no trouble whisking our three, Craven coaches, and a four-wheel van, along the double-track branch,

There was some interesting and quite vintage rolling stock in service in Cork.

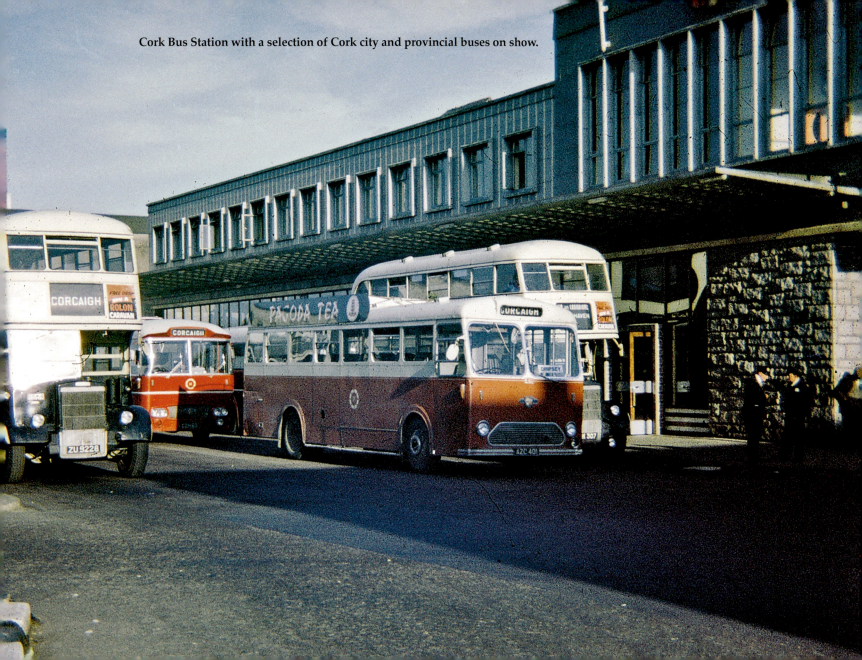
Cork Bus Station with a selection of Cork city and provincial buses on show.

stopping at all stations, but not at Cobh Junction, where the 20-mile Youghal Branch split off. Youghal, a popular seaside escape for Cork folk, boasted CIE camping carriages in 1969, and brought in mobs of visitors from the city on excursion specials on summer holidays and bank holidays, but it wasn't worth visiting, as I'd have to use the replacement bus on an ordinary weekday. A quick look around Cobh Station and Quay, as our loco ran round its carriages, revealed the large customs hall and booking office, used by trans-Atlantic passengers. It was a moving thought that thousands of destitute Irish immigrants, fleeing poverty and oppression in Ireland especially after an Gorta Mor, the Great Hunger of 1844-1848, sailed off from there to a new life in America. Cobh Station and Quay was redolent with history, even though, by 1969, the last liner had called, leaving memories of the dead of the *Lusitania*, laid out on the quay after her sinking in 1915, and up to 400 ships calling during the port's heyday in the 1920s. Today, there has been a revival in fortunes, with cruise ships using Cobh's deep-water quay and renewed *Titanic* interest, and the railway is doing well.

Our train left at 14.20 and I was back in Cork at 14.47. I called in at the Bord Failte office to book a B&B for the night, and I was given an address up St Patrick's Hill whose 25% gradient certainly kept Corkonians fit, even if their accent was as hard for me to fathom as mine was for them. They kept asking me how things were up in Belfast, a city that most in Cork had hardly heard of or had any interest in, given that July 1969 was still a few weeks before the Troubles kicked off in Derry in August that year. The North was another country down there.

Accommodation secured, it was off on a CIE Leyland double decker to Blarney, where I just had to kiss the famous stone – you can judge for yourself if it worked! I was also keen to see if there were any remains of the late-lamented, 3ft gauge Cork & Muskerry Railway, closed in 1934, and which our bus was replacing, but I drew a blank on that, failing miserably to spot the surviving station building at Blarney.

The C&MR shared tracks with Cork trams, on its way out of the city, and, not for the first time on the trip, I longed for a time

It was a slog up St Patrick's Hill to my B&B in Cork!

B147 waits at Cobh with my train back to Cork.

machine or even thought that being born sooner it would have been great to have ridden on this line, the West Cork, the Cork trams and the other narrow gauge line, serving the city, the Cork Blackrock & Passage Railway. But I was too late and, in 1969, few Irish people were concerned about local railway heritage. The past was the past.

I was sitting in the summer sunshine waiting for the bus back to Cork, when some French tourists appeared and began, rudely, loudly and cheekily, to discuss me in some detail, including why I was wearing a combat jacket, then very fashionable for young bucks like me. Was I soldier? Was I in the IRA? What was I? Was I, loosely translated from French, a thick Mick? And all in French.

They got the shock of their lives when I answered in French, as I'd taken the subject up to Scottish Higher and English A level standard at school and had just passed it in first year at Glasgow University. I told them where to go in my dreadfully-accented French, as these were the days when you were taught to read and write the language efficiently, but, as for speaking it, oh dear.

I probably sounded aggressively guttural to them, but, in any case, it had the desired effect and they fled. *"Les Francais merde!"* to my great shame, probably did it. It must have been something to do with kissing the Blarney stone…….

But back on the bus to Cork, a smooth, pleasant run, a dander up O'Connell Street, which, like Dublin boasted a Wellworths and a Penny's, and a feeling that this was a busy city which served its hinterland well. After a Wimpey Bar meal, very trendy in 1969, it was a drag up the hill to my digs, where a very friendly landlady, who, it turned out, had a cousin in Donegal, was able to tell me that a train ran every morning on the Cork City Railways, around 10.00 am, and, if I'd time, as I was interested in railways, I shouldn't miss it. *"It's quite a sight,"* she said. *"I don't drive down there when the train is on the street!"*

Wednesday 9th July:
"Out the fecking' way!" and off to Tralee

After breakfast, there was plenty of time to wander down St Patrick's Hill to Kent Station, drop my suitcase at the left luggage, and follow the Cork City Railway tracks back towards Albert Quay Station, once the Cork Bandon & South Coast Railway terminus, and still in use as a goods depot. I was in plenty of time to witness my landlady's promised goods train battling with the heavy and slightly wild, Cork traffic, mostly against the flow on a one-way system, not forgetting crossing two opening bridges across the River Lee. I'd seen pictures of the line in action in steam days, and was looking forward to a diesel-hauled train doing battle.

Just before 10.00 am, a black-livered C218, a Bo-Bo, diesel electric, built in the UK in 1957, with a Crossley engine and Metrovick equipment, as part of the CIE dieselisation project, began to poke its nose, without any high-viz markings, out of the gates of Albert Quay Station, some flat wagons, evilly-black-looking bitumen tankers and a brakevan in tow.

A Cork city services Atlantean, engine screaming, scuttled past the front of the loco, anxious to be safely out of the way, and then, the fun began! The driver of C218 opened his charge up, with a satisfying engine roar and plenty of exhaust fumes, as a railwayman, devoid of a semblance of uniform and without a flag, ran in front of the train, shooing possibly suicidal car drivers out of the way. The railway factotum looked anxiously back, from time to time, to ensure that the train wasn't threatening to get too close to him, either. He was a good runner. CIE, clearly, kept him pretty fit. Occasionally, he yelled *"Out the fecking way!"* towards any vehicle, cyclist or pedestrian looking as if they were foolish enough to jostle for road space with C218 in full flight.

The train rumbled over the two lifting bridges, missed several cars and another bus, without anyone batting an eyelid, as this was normal life on Cork city roads where drivers, many of whom,

A CIE Atlantean gets well out of the way as C 218 makes ready to leave Albert Quay Station to do battle with cars, lorries and buses on the Cork City Railway.

Pause for breath as a van is filled up at the Esso station beside the tracks.

quite legally, in 1969, hadn't sat a driving test if they'd learned before 1964. I kept up with the train, but everyone involved, especially the front runner, had a welcome break as the track was blocked alongside a fully-functioning Esso petrol station, which required vehicles filling up to straddle the tracks, and that was exactly what a Chro-Mesh van was doing. The white-coated, petrol station attendant, yes, there were such people in 1969, and little self-service, seemed to be taking as much time as possible to fill up the van, while our train man stood, hands on hips, waiting patiently. I got the impression that this was not the first time the stand-off between rail and road had taken place at this spot.

Once the van finally drove off, C218, with much healthy engine noise bouncing off the walls of the buildings, scraped by in Brian Boru Street cutting, and headed for the gates into Kent Station's goods yard. It had been quite a sight, street theatre on the 5ft 3in gauge, and one that continued until final closure of Albert Quay Station and the tracks through the city streets in 1976.

This street running, which dated from the opening of the line in 1911, was more than worth seeing, and, the 18 year-old me, saw it as one of the last vestiges of Ireland's railways which charged up main streets along and across roads without warning, such as the Clogher Valley, the Tralee & Dingle and Cork's own Cork & Muskerry Light Railway. The visit to Cork had been a real highlight of the trip.

Honour satisfied, it was time for a quick snack in the station buffet, and on to Tralee by the 13.30. At the head of our Cravens carriages, was a General Motors Bo-Bo, a double-ended B class, ticking over with purpose and intent, in readiness to tackle the standing start from the platform end, up the fierce gradient though the three-quarters-of-a-mile-long, Glanmire Tunnel, where damp rails had often brought trains to a standstill, especially in steam days.

But, we made it through and up to Kilbarry, as our driver thrashed the loco, the howl of its engine, working hard, echoing off the tunnel walls. With smart running, we were into Mallow for 14.04, and, this being a through train for Tralee, meant that there was no need to change there.

Off onto the scenic, and single, Kerry line, with much train staff exchanging, all by hand, we were booked to serve Banteer, Millstreet, Rathmore and Killarney which was, and is, the tourist honeypot, much developed by the railways since trains reached it in 1853, and, in 1969, the destination of CIE's popular Radio Train, which piped entertainment and information to passengers throughout the train, from an on-board studio.

At Killarney, our train had to run into the former terminal station there, and back out onto the main line, before setting out for Tralee. All great stuff with signalling, hand-signals and much gesturing by platform staff, and, I recall a very large and loud 'Yank' proclaiming, as we reversed out, *"Gee, we're going back to Cork!"* The guard was able to assure him that all was well.

On, then, in brilliant sunshine, for Farranfore, once the junction for the fabled and wonderfully-scenic, Valencia Harbour Branch, which, sadly, had closed in 1960, before my time. Yet again, I yearned for that time machine. But, to the credit of CIE, the replacement bus service, the ghost of the Valencia Branch train, timed to connect with the main line service, was waiting, and as my railway timetable showed, CIE was much better than BR at maintaining connections in and out of replacement bus services on closed branch lines, years after the actual closure. It was probably easier because CIE ran the trains and buses themselves, providing an integrated transport system years before the idea became fashionable, but sadly, today, rarely attainable in mainland Britain.

Farranfore, with its abandoned bay platform for the Valentia train, would be the departure point for me, my wife and our three sons in August 1988, for a day trip to Dublin, a real bargain at just 19 Punts, when, on holiday on the Dingle peninsula, we decided to visit the capital, then celebrating its millennium. In 1969, I had no inkling of the changes that would revolutionise my life in the short years ahead, in the shape of graduation in 1972, a career, marriage in 1975, three children by 1982, and a daughter after that! How fleeting is youth…

Leaving Kent Station for Tralee.

If you'd told carefree me, sitting happily in a CIE carriage, all of that in 1969, I wouldn't have believed you. I was enjoying a wonderfully free, and carefree time in my life that seemed to go on for ever, when Irish railways were the life for me and when girls were for the post-study era. I suspect that, in those days, despite it being the swinging sixties, I wasn't that different from lots of lads my age. It was a great period in my life, and writing this has made it accessible all over again.

At Tralee Casement Station, time was short, as I was catching the 17.00 to Dublin, and we had arrived from Cork at 16.10. So, it was down to the shed, with its turntable and water tower, to see what locos were there, followed by a failed attempt to smoke out some of the remains of the fabled Tralee & Dingle Railway. All I could do was look west towards the beckoning Slieve Mish Mountains, and imagine the T&D trains, bravely battling through them.

At the shed, which still served the then, freight-only, North Kerry Line to Limerick, I found friendly and helpful staff who were happy to show me three locos in the shape of B class 124, which was preparing to come off shed to couple up to my Dublin train, C212, shunting the yard, and the loco off the Radio Train, waiting to return to Killarney. Tralee Station, serving the busy county town of Kerry, boasted a fine display of semaphore signals and a loading gauge as traditional goods traffic was in full flow. All that was missing was a steam engine, and, as I found, right across the CIE system, at that time, it was all very much like a working museum in action, a very traditional railway, with modern motive power grafted on.

Back on the 17.00 through train to Dublin, I had plenty of time to see the stations go by, and, then on to the Dublin-Cork main line at Mallow for the non-stop trip north and east to Dublin. I was pretty hungry, by this time, and having done an urgent recce of the cash left, and remember that, in 1969, you couldn't pop along to an ATM, I decided I had enough – just – to cover my digs for three more nights in Dublin, plus one in Dundalk, with some money for food.

So, financially reassured, I made for the restaurant car and tucked into a superb steak and chips, which, if I remember right, cost 12/6, a fortune to student me, but very reasonable for what you got, as the food was freshly cooked in the tiny kitchen space in the dining car. Again, plenty of silverware, stewards in white jackets and a whiff of Edwardian splendour as we glided along over the well-maintained track of CIE's prestige main line. And, this time, despite my worst fears, and being geared up for a barney, if need be, the steward issued me with the correct value ticket receipt from his TIM ticket machine, and couldn't have been more pleasant. My faith in CIE train catering staff was restored.

I can't remember anything more about that journey up to Dublin, and I have to confess that I probably dozed off, before waking up about Kildare, and was pleased to see Dublin when we arrived at Heuston at 21.10. I think I'd found that there is an endurance limit, even for keen, 18 year-old railway fans such as me!

I was soon back in the same B&B on the North Circular that I'd been in at the start of my week, and, after a great welcome, tea and scones, from the landlady, who, now thought of me as a temporary son, staggered off to bed, to prepare for the rest of the days to come on the tracks. Just lying snoozing in the July sun on Murvagh Beach in Donegal seemed like a good idea. This rail pilgrimage was turning out to be harder work than I'd thought….

Tralee with a B class heading my train back to Dublin.

On Tralee Shed, B and C class locos await their turn of duty.

B165 Radio Train loco at Tralee.

Thursday 10th July: From the Bustle of Dublin to rural Loughrea – and the Legion of Mary!

The next day I was up early for my Ulster Fry, for I had to get across Dublin by bus and make for Pearse Station, named after Padraig himself, and formerly Westland Row, to catch the 08.40 for Galway. That, according to the timetable, would take me along the former Midland Great Western line to Attymon Junction. There, I would board the train for Loughrea, and experience the last, traditional branch line still working in Ireland in 1969. That just couldn't be missed.

Although a through station, Westland Row had a feeling of trains going somewhere, and I was keen to travel over the old MGWR main line as it headed west into the fastness of the midlands. A double ended B class General Motors diesel hummed away purposefully at the head of our eight-coach train, which included a buffet car and a mail van. The atmosphere was one of importance and bustle, that romantic notion of travelling by train that has been lost on today's formulaic railway.

Off, then, after much slamming of carriage doors, platform staff whistles, and an answering toot from up front, we were away out through suburban service, Tara Street, and over the elevated section, with its views of Dublin from above, to Connolly. We ran through it with an air of importance, and out past North Strand Junction, Drumcondra and Glasnevin, towards Liffey Junction, in those days, stuffed with cattle wagons and freight trains, with the line down to Broadstone, the former MGWR terminus, easy to pick out.

From there, the B class engine howled away as we ran alongside the banks of the Royal Canal all the way to Mullingar. This had the feel of a real main line train on a real main line, and it was made much more exciting as we charged through the loops as I could see the snatcherman, the driver's assistant, leaning perilously out of the cab, as the loco rollicked and rolled, to extend the electric train staff exchange apparatus arm, and swap the staff with the mechanical ground apparatus at block posts. That, allied with plenty of wheel noise, engine roar and a swaying train, left me with the feeling of adventurous railway travel, as I read names such as Leixlip, Maynooth, home to the national Catholic seminary, still, in 1969 churning out priests for home and export, and the romantically-named, remote 46th Mile Box, just four miles from Mullingar, then an important junction for the Sligo and Galway lines.

At Mullingar, reached 09.53, we sat for six, frenzied minutes as the signalman delivered the train staff for the section ahead, passengers left and joined, parcels and mails were taken off, and the buffet car steward hung out of the window enjoying his fag as he

Running over the impressive Shannon Viaduct into Athlone.

Attymon Junction – the perfect rural junction.

took it all in. He nodded to the wheel tapper whose hammer rung on the coach wheel rims, as the tapper, clearly happy that he could listen to his work while talking, gave up, a *"How are ye?"* to the smoker above him.

The old MGWR main line west is now a greenway for cyclists and walkers, and it's hard to realise that this was an important, trunk railway route, before CIE hit on the idea of sending Galway-Dublin trains via Portarlington. But, in July 1969, we fairly surged westwards toward Athlone, though flat and boggy land, much of which you couldn't see thanks to high hedges on either side of the track.

We reached Athlone, the dead centre of Ireland, and home to Radio Athlone, enjoyed by many Irish exiles in Britain, our family included, its call sign, the opening notes of *O'Donnell Abu*, connecting people to home. Now, here it was, the legendary town, which had seen much action during the War of Independence, an important Irish army barracks, and the junction for Westport, Galway, Mullingar and Portarlington.

My reading had told me that it was here that the Midland Great Western met with its rival, the Great Southern and Western Railway, both companies having their own stations, while we entered the MGWR station, for Galway, after crossing the impressive 542-foot-long Shannon Bridge, opened in 1851, painted in white, with an opening span. This was a real railway town.

We arrived 10.38, to a repeat of the frenzy at Mullingar, for it was clear that CIE prided itself in smart train working, and were off at 10.44, with my timetable telling me that we would stop at Attymon Junction at 11.27, to change there for the 11.40 to Loughrea. There was plenty of slack in the connection at Attymon, with time to have a look around.

And there it was: a fully-functioning, traditional, rural railway, junction station, once common in Ireland and Britain, complete with branch platform at which sat our train headed by C202, pulling the line's unique passenger carriage, which came complete with electric storage heaters for winter use, and three vans. This was a real mixed train, the very stuff of branch lines.

I had put a lot of store at finding the essence of that real, Irish branch line on the Loughrea Branch, for, on all of my journeys, so far, *Irish Railways Today*, listed a litany of long-gone junctions and branches closed in the late 50s or early 60s. That was when CIE enthusiastically wielded its version of Beeching's axe, and, in the classic fashion of the day, choking off feeder traffic to the main line, even though bus replacement services were always provided.

But, I needn't have been disappointed, for the driver, seeing me with my BR Intercity bag – very trendy at the time – asked if I'd like to join him on the footplate. *"Up ye come, son,"* he said, *"and I'll tell you all about this road."*

The view from the cab over the well-kept Loughrea Branch line towards Dunsandle

Looking for all the world like a model, C202 sits at Loughrea.

So, as the coach sides vibrated in time to the revolutions of the C 202's engine, as we waited time, the driver, very much a steam man who came late to diesel, gave me all the gen on the line. He ran through its history, exciting days during the War of Independence and the Civil War, running out of coal in the Second World War, better known down south as 'The Emergency', the branch's importance to the cattle trade, and his wonder that it was still running.

Off, then, up the branch, the track well-kept with a drainage trench down the middle of the ballast, as we ran alongside drystone walls with some scrubby fields beyond. The sense of remoteness and being far from the main line bustle of Dublin was palpable, as we halted for a couple of passengers to leave and four to join at the intermediate station of Dunsandle, before hefting on up the grade to Loughrea, the driver pointing out the mileposts to me on the 9-mile run up from the junction.

Loughrea was the essential branch terminus, itself, and almost looked like a full scale model, with run-round loop, goods and engine sheds, a ground frame shelter, with the electric train staff apparatus in the stationmaster's office, turntable, and a cattle loading bank, holding a long line of cattle wagons, for this was fair day.

As it was 12.20, I was getting pretty hungry and asked the driver where he recommended. He pointed me in the direction of the best lunch in the village at the eating rooms frequented by the cattle

A long line of cattle wagons awaits the fair traffic as C202 gets ready to run round. A CIE bus and coach sit by the trees.

dealers, and in I went. The place was full of large scale dealers and farmers, the food was hearty and portions gigantic to suit the clientele, and I enjoyed one of those classic Irish lunches of turkey and ham, with mounds of cabbage and floury potatoes. This was the days before everyone started to demand foreign and exotic flavours; in Loughrea in 1969, traditional Irish cooking was king. The portions were so large, that I as an 18 year-old, who ate like a horse, didn't need a dinner that night, back in Dublin!

I had plenty of time to take a look round the town, as buying and selling went on, and, back at the station, the stationmaster said that there would be a cattle special going out that evening. It was hard to realise that by 1975, both the Loughrea Branch and CIE cattle trains would be history, so much was the line worn into the culture of the town. As one of the cattle dealers told me over lunch: "*We'd be lost without the railway.*" By the time the branch closed, cattle by rail was fading fast, with local slaughter houses in rural parts of Ireland and refrigerator lorries taking over. The days of sending live cattle exports out of the Irish Midlands, some to Britain, were coming to an end, as dealers embraced change, having been rail-dependent for well over a century.

Back on the train, the 15.35 departure to Attymon Junction, I enjoyed the return jaunt, and at 16.25, I boarded the Dublin train, all pomp and circumstance, compared to the wee, Loughrea one. I don't recall too much of the journey in a Park Royal coach, as it was hot, I'd had a large lunch, rail fatigue had taken over, and, I must have nodded off.

But, this train offered me the chance to go right through to Dun Laoghaire Pier, where it connected with the BR sailing for Holyhead, with connections on to London. This was the main train of the day from Galway, and it was a route well-known to Irish exiles, seeking a new life in England.

It was clear that quite a few younger passengers weren't on holiday like myself, but were making the journey across the sea to new lives, and, as we arrived into Connolly at 19.11, I noticed a contingent from the Legion of Mary on the platform, waiting to board.

Their mission was to talk to young exiles making for England, firstly, to try to talk them out of going, but, if they insisted, to give them contact details for Legion help and support in London to ensure that they didn't come to harm in the Big Smoke. In 1969, this was still De Valera's Ireland, and, although change was happening slowly, the Catholic Church was very much in charge.

I was happily lost in a reverie about travelling over the first railway in Ireland to Dun Laoghaire Pier on this important boat train, when I was asked by a lady in her later years, leaning over me.

"*Are ye running off to London, son?*" she fired off at me. "*Think of yer mammy back home, think of all the dangers of the city. Why don't ye go back home and turn round before ye get on the boat?*"

I started to explain to her that I was on holiday and enjoying a bit of train travel, but she would have none of it, mistaking my Glasgow Irish accent for a northerner. "*Ye's from the North, then, son?*" she asked. "*What are ye running away from?*"

At this point I took out my rambler ticket to show her that I was not going to London, nor running away, and she began to back off, seeming to even believe me, and she moved on to another target in the shape of two cheeky Dublin gels further up the carriage from me, and they had a right good barney with her.

CIE gave the Legion members free travel to and from Dun Laoghaire on the boat trains, and there was no doubt that their intention was of the best: it was just that the lady who chinned me thought I was at it. And, no, I didn't go to Dublin, and did go home to my Mammy in Donegal later that week when the cash started to run out. Irish emigration was still far too high in 1969, and, sadly, much of the traffic on the Galway-Dun Laoghaire boat train was one-way.

Back in my Dublin digs, I planned the next day down the east coast to the post of Rosslare, hopeful that the Legion of Mary wouldn't track me towards the port there, just in case they thought I was trying to make my escape via Fishguard!

Friday 11th July Railcars To Rosslare

On a very sunny Friday morning, I presented myself at Pearse for the 09.00 to Rosslare Harbour, where an AEC railcar set sat with engines idling. Once aboard, it was back down the Dublin and Kingston Railway track through Dun Laoghaire, to Bray, the railcars giving a good account of themselves over the flat and scenic line along the coast. I spotted the Martello Tower of James Joyce fame – I'd studied *Dubliners* at university that year – and marvelled at the wealthy homes of of Killiney. But, as we began to climb, for real, towards Bray Head, the railcar gearboxes bustling away to melodious downward changes, and through its tunnels, with the railway clinging to a ledge above the sea on a route originally designed by no less a person that Isambard Kingdom Brunel himself, I became even more impressed. This was real railwaying on the eastern edge of Ireland.

Inland, then towards Rathdrum, through pleasant scenery, and down to Enniscorthy, where, at 11.09, we crossed the up railcar set, the signalman standing between the trains to juggle the electric train staffs, there being no snatchers on this line. I duly hung out to catch such a characteristic, bustling scene of the railway in 1969, and, when I came back to my seat, the lady across the table from

My AEC railcar set for Rosslare gets ready to leave Pearse Station.

Our train crossed the up railcar working for Dublin at Enniscorthy. The signalman stands between the trains sorting out the electric train staffs for the single lines.

me, said, in an educated Dublin accent: *"Do you like the trains, son?"*

As she obviously wasn't an undercover Legion of Mary spy – I was getting paranoid(!) – we struck up a conversation about the railway, life in general, where I was from – and, no she'd never been to Donegal or Glasgow, but lived very happily in her Dublin-south eastern world – and was Church of Ireland, and very Anglified in speech and mannerism. Kindly, she asked if I was missing home and my Mammy. I reminded her of her own son, she smiled. She was probably in her late 40s, on reflection, but at 18, I reckoned that she very old!

I assured her that I wasn't missing my Mammy, and would be seeing her in two days' time, and we both enjoyed the chat, the scenery and the journey together, until she bid me good luck and farewell as she got off at Wexford, where she was visiting a friend. What a lovely lady she was, warm and friendly, as were most passengers I met on my travels in the Ireland of 1969.

After Wexford O'Hanrahan, the fun really started, for our train negotiated the quayside, squeezing past cars, as we made for Wexford South on a piece of unfenced railway as good as anything the Cork City Railways offered, except that this was the Dublin-Rosslare main line. As *Irish Railways Today* put it:

> Negotiation of this stretch of line is often made more difficult for train drivers by motorists parking their vehicles too close to the running line.

We did make it, only just, and here was a piece of line of character which made you wonder what the original builders were thinking of when they built it, although there were no cars when it opened in 1872. The good news is that it is still in use today and very much worth a trip.

On, then, over an exposed section of track with stout, rock, sea defences, to Rosslare Harbour, where we arrived at 12.15, and a look around this busy port which had its origins in the English Great Western Railway's Irish ambitions on its Fishguard-Rosslare route. The steamers were now run by British Railways but, it was time to catch the 18.00 for Waterford, via Wellington Bridge, a through boat train to Cork, change at Waterford at 19.05, and travel via Kilkenny and Carlow, home of the Irish Sugar Company's factory. In 1969, it boasted its own sidings and locos which came into their own in the sugar beet season, and up to Kildare, where we joined the manline for Dublin Heuston, arriving there at 21.55.

It had been an epic day out, and although I saw plenty of CIE lines and operation in the south east, it was a hot day, and I dozed through large parts of the journey, proving that even the most hardened rail fan has limits! Tomorrow, Saturday 12 July, an auspicious date over the border, beckoned, as I looked forward to sampling the legendary Great Northern Railway of Ireland lines, the company that had made such a lasting impression on me as a wee boy, when we made the epic journey by GNR train from Belfast to Bundoran in 1957.

Squeezing along Wexford Quay past the cars on the main line to Rosslare. The gents on the bench have a great view of the train!

Pearse Station, the Dublin terminus for Rosslare line trains.

The driver leaves his former GNR (I) 'BUT' railcar set at Howth to take his break. Howth is now served by DART electric trains.

Saturday 12th July: Ghosts of the GNR and Crossing the Boyne on the 12th!

Friday was a bit of an epic, but I was determined to get my final day's money's worth out of my rambler ticket, so it was Dublin–Howth by ex-GNR railcar, a 'BUT', just as I had travelled on from Belfast to Omagh in the years after the Bundoran line was axed by the Stormont Government, and we had to change from the train to an uncomfortable Ulster Transport Authority replacement bus to reach the Atlantic resort.

Now, passed to CIE when the Great Northern Railway Board was abolished in 1958, the railcar no longer carried the former glories of its GNR (I) Oxford blue-and-cream livery, but was turned out in CIE black-and-tan. Still, it was pure GNR inside, just as I'd remembered, and made all the right noises, and, if I shut my eyes, I could imagine that I was on that Omagh train, somewhere among the bushes of County Tyrone, before the Derry Road was cruelly axed by Stormont in 1965.

Howth itself, was well-known in our family lore, as my parents had taken my big sister there on holiday before I'd arrived in 1950, and they would tell me all about the Hill of Howth Tramway, whose remains I spotted at Sutton, where there was a superb GNR signal cabin and signals, and at Howth itself. But, of course, like all the best aspects of the Irish railway system, I seemed to have managed to miss them by a few years. The tramway closed in 1958, and more's the pity.

Back at Connolly, there was, a bonus, as I caught sight of the former Sligo, Leitrim & Northern Counties railcar B, sold to CIE, when the SL&NCR closed in 1957, in the carriage sidings. As it was such a rare vehicle, I blew one frame of slide film on it, even though it was far away. Photography, then, was very different from today's digital profligacy.

I took a CIE railcar set north to Dundalk, former Great Northern epicentre, where its Mills-designed, brick station still spoke of the company's great days, and where its extensive works was situated. With GNR stations largely intact, GNR signal cabins working, and

The classic Great Northern signalling, crossing gates and signal box at Sutton.

the railway much as it was, it felt very different from CIE down south, even though some CIE coaching stock was in use and its General Motors diesels were common currency.

Best of all was sitting behind the driver as we swung round the curve from Drogheda and out onto the impressive Boyne Viaduct, I could see the gauntleted track, installed when the viaduct was rebuilt in 1932 and strengthened for the fabled GNR compound locos to cross on its fastest Belfast-Dublin expresses. And I laughed to myself, for here was I, a Catholic, crossing the River Boyne on the 12th Day of July. Whatever would they think back home?!

Dundalk still carried an air of importance, and you could see the remains of the Irish North line towards Clones, again, a victim of the Stormont Government policy of withdrawing railways east of the Bann. I was thrilled at how much of the GNR spirit lingered around the place.

Back down in Drogheda, I took time to photograph the Boyne Viaduct from the green grassy banks themselves, and, again on the 12th. I made up for it by visiting St Peter's Drogheda which displays the head of (then Blessed, now Saint) Oliver Plunkett, in a popular shrine. It was once served by GNR pilgrimage specials to honour the distant relative of the Dougherty clan, who was martyred by being hanged, drawn and quartered at Tyburn in London for his faith in 1681.

Then it was off back down to Dublin, before heading north, one last time on the 16.20 from Connolly to Dundalk, to overnight there, but not before visiting the legendary Dolphin Records shop in Talbot Street to buy my first Wolfe Tones LP, *The Rifles of the IRA*, celebrating the original IRA's exploits in the War of Independence. I made sure I buried it in my suitcase before I crossed the border the next day, just in case the northern customs man didn't find it to his taste! Maybe all 18 year-old were rebels in 1969, one way or another. I was probably just conforming.

Heading north near Gormanstown, looking out from my ex-GNR(I), now CIE, railcar set, as the down Northern Ireland Railways Enterprise express is about to pass. It is made up of a '70' Class diesel electric railcar set, heading for Dublin on this fine, racing stretch of main line track.

Crossing the Boyne on the Twelfth Day of July, of all days! The view from the AEC railcar car shows the gauntleted tracks across the bridge which provides a vital link on the Dublin-Belfast main line.

Bonus at Connolly. The ex-Sligo Leitrim & Northern Counties railcar B, repainted in black-and-tan livery, sits in the sidings. CIE used it both in service and for driver training and it survives, awaiting restoration at the Downpatrick Railway.

International trains at Dublin Connolly as a Northern Ireland Railways 70 class railcar Enterprise set sits on the centre road, ready to return to Belfast, and a CIE Howth suburban set gets ready to leave. The CIE C class loco at the left was shunting the yard.

Sunday 13th July – Homewards Bound

Even then, and remember that the Troubles of August 1969, had yet to break out, Dundalk was an edgy, Republican town. I stayed in a B&B, and headed for Mass on the Sunday morning, before picking up the 11.33, Sundays only, slow train for Belfast Great Victoria Street, there being no Enterprise expresses on Sundays.

After Mass the priest came out of the church to bless the local IRA colour party, who had been at Mass, and had been praised in the sermon, and they drilled and stood to attention. As a young man of hopeless unrealistic, armchair Republican views, nurtured by romantic rebel tunes and my father's politics, I was impressed. But, approached by one of the party to be asked: *"So yer from Glasgow then, son, a good Donegal man too. How would ye like to join?"* I decided not to take up the offer, and, in the light of all the heartbreak that happened, far from my dangerous romanticism of youth, it was just as well that I didn't. How much worse would the Troubles have been if there had been social media, and radicalisation in those days?

Back on track, my train was a CIE set, which included some GNR coaches, and there was a definite thrill of crossing the border, my guidebook telling me to look out for the border post between Mountpleasant and Adavoyle, an area which became notorious for attacks on trains during the 70s.

We stopped at Portadown old station, which was still there in 1969, and, just before it, I could see the course of the closed Derry Road and the line to Armagh and Clones, and wondered if my trips over the Derry Road as a wee boy had really happened.

There were brief stops at Lurgan and Lisburn, too, and the track was in need of some TLC, as this was a low point in the life of the cruelly-cropped railways in the north, and then we proceeded with a rattle of chains from underneath, plenty of roaring rail noise, and a strange two-and-fro motion, all of which spoke of a need for investment.

Arrival at Great Victoria Street meant the customs men, but they didn't bother me and my LP remained safe. It was sad to see the

Sadly-depleted Belfast Great Victoria Street Station, well past its heyday, with Northern Ireland Railways then new Enterprise train, in July 1970, a year after Hugh arrived there in 1969.

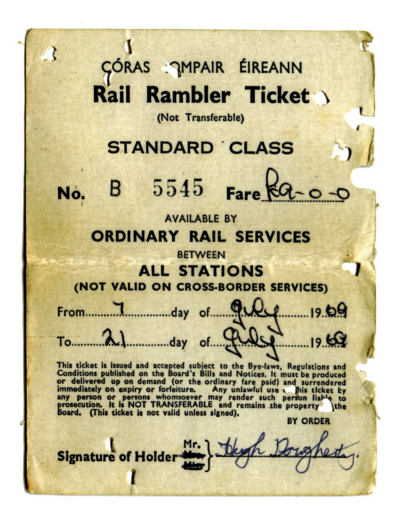

With the scars of its journey the well traveled rambler ticket.

station at which my Dad had shown me the GNR map and our far-off destination of Bundoran, much reduced from its former glory. A large part had been hived off to create a bus station, to house the rail replacement services, and it was clear that the once-magnificent GNR terminus, pride of the line, was on its last legs. It was all so different from the railway scene down south, which bustled, and, despite political debates raging in the Dail about the future of the railways, there was a feeling that the worst of the cuts were over, and staff morale, judging by the staff I met on my travels, was high.

Back in our holiday home at Ballykillowen, reached via a Northern Ireland Railways diesel multiple unit to Derry Waterside, a joint CDR/CIE bus to Laghey and a suitcase-in-hand two mile tramp up a country road, a very tired me delivered a present of a bar of Irish coffee chocolate to my parents, not forgetting a week's washing, especially for my Mammy, and regaled them with carefully-edited tales of my 1,522 miles on the 5ft 3in gauge, and all for £9.

It's hard to realise that my rail pilgrimage is well over 50 years ago now, in a very different, and, dare I say it, a more 'Irish' Ireland, before Europe, before the internet, before the impact of the Celtic Tiger, and before the Catholic Church lost its supremacy and before the subsequent seismic changes in Irish society.

The railway that I rode on, served that society. It was very recognisable from steam days, with plenty of Victorian technology in daily use, manning levels high, goods trains sharing the tracks with passenger trains, and eccentricities such as Cork City Railways. I'm so glad that I saw all that I did, viewed through the wide-open and romantic eyes of an 18 year-old, let loose on the world for the first time, for the Irish railways of today are efficient, and up there with the best of any world systems, but the character of what I experienced in 1969, is largely gone.

I hope that you have enjoyed my journey back in time. It's been a journey of rediscovery for me. And I'm still glad that I avoided 'capture' by the Legion of Mary!

I might have been in Dun Laoghaire yet……

Journey's end by rail: Waterside Station in Derry, for the bus on to Donegal.